A Whole New World

by Barbara Fifer

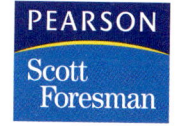

PEARSON
Scott Foresman

Editorial Offices: Glenview, Illinois • Parsippany, New Jersey • New York, New York

Sales Offices: Needham, Massachusetts • Duluth, Georgia • Glenview, Illinois
Coppell, Texas • Sacramento, California • Mesa, Arizona

What Is out There?

In the 1300s traders from Europe were interested in the spices and treasures of India and China. Spices were worth as much as gold. They helped keep food fresh and taste better.

By the late 1400s **explorers** hoped to sail ships to India and China. The **explorers** had to find the way and draw maps.

Explorers hoped to find spices.

Explorers used ships on their journeys.

Portugal

Africa was one of the first places that explorers went. Sailors from Portugal traveled down Africa's west coast in the early 1400s. Portugal hoped to start **colonies** there.

Christopher Columbus explored for Spain.

Christopher Columbus

Christopher Columbus was an Italian explorer. He wanted to sail west to find a new way to get to China.

Columbus sailed across the Atlantic Ocean. He reached land on October 12, 1492. He was sure he was near China — but he was in the Americas!

John Cabot

John Cabot was another Italian explorer. King Henry VII of England sent Cabot across the Atlantic Ocean in 1497 in search of spices.

Cabot sailed to what is now Canada. Cabot tried to return there the next year with a **fleet**, or group of ships. One ship turned back, and the others disappeared.

John Cabot sailed for England.

The Taino lived on islands in the Caribbean Sea.

Spain

Spain claimed land and started colonies. Columbus left men behind on his first trip. The men fought with the Taino.

The colonists made the Taino work for them. Colonists also demanded gold or silver from the Taino. Soon, ships carrying this treasure were sailing across the Atlantic Ocean.

Robbers!

Robbers soon heard about the ships that were carrying treasure from the New World. There were two types of robbers. Privateers were people hired by a king or queen to steal **cargo** from ships of other countries. Pirates were outlaws, or thieves, who stole on their own.

Sir Francis Drake was an explorer and privateer. He sailed around the world from 1577–1580.

Juan Rodríguez Cabrillo

Juan Rodríguez Cabrillo helped the Spanish military explore new lands. In 1542 Cabrillo led an expedition up the coast of today's California. He is remembered for being the first European to explore California.

Juan Rodríguez Cabrillo explored California.

Jacques Cartier explored North America.

Jacques Cartier

In 1535 King Francis I of France sent Jacques Cartier to explore North America. Cartier made three trips to what is now Canada and sailed up the St. Lawrence River. He claimed the land for France.

Francisco Vásquez de Coronado

Explorers from Spain moved into the American Southwest from Mexico. In 1540 Francisco Vásquez de Coronado took three hundred Spanish men and eight hundred American Indians with him as he explored what is now Arizona, New Mexico, Texas, Oklahoma, and Kansas.

Missionaries such as Father Junípero Serra later reached California. They began building missions in 1769.

Francisco Vásquez de Coronado explored the American Southwest.

Hernando de Soto explored the Mississippi River.

The Spanish and the French Explore

In 1541 Spain's Hernando de Soto was the first European to explore the Mississippi River. He and his men wanted to find gold and **conquer** the land and people who lived there.

Louis Jolliet and Jacques Marquette explored most of the river's northern half for France in 1673. In 1682 another French explorer, Robert La Salle, traveled the entire river.

Samuel de Champlain explored for France.

Samuel de Champlain

Samuel de Champlain explored for France. In 1603 Champlain sailed to what is now Canada. He found Ottawa River, Lake Ontario, Lake Huron, and Lake Champlain. Champlain started a colony that is now Québec, Canada.

Henry Hudson

Henry Hudson was English but sailed for the Dutch in 1609. Hudson crossed the Atlantic to look for a **strait** that went to China. A strait is a narrow body of water connecting two larger ones.

Hudson sailed up the Hudson River to Albany, in New York State. He started a Dutch colony there.

Henry Hudson sailed for the Dutch.

Early Colonies

English traders started their country's first permanent colony, Jamestown, Virginia, in 1607.

In 1624 the Dutch began the New Netherland Colony in New York, New Jersey, Connecticut, and Delaware. The Dutch bought Manhattan Island from the American Indians and built a town. Later, England took control of the town and named it New York.

Sweden's colony in Delaware started in 1638. The Dutch took it over later, and then England.

Jamestown was England's first permanent colony.

Colonists had to plant crops.

Why Explore?

Explorers sailed on long journeys. Some explorers ran out of food or got sick, and some fought in battles. Explorers traveled because they worked for a country or a company. Some wanted to know more about the world. Others wanted fame and riches.

Glossary

cargo a group of things a ship takes from one place to another

colony a country or area that is ruled by another country

conquer to take control, by force, of people and the land where they live

explorer a person who travels looking for new lands and discoveries

fleet a large group of ships

strait a narrow body of water connecting two larger bodies of water